BUILD A BETTER YOU

FOR TEENS

This edition was published by The Dreamwork Collective

The Dreamwork Collective LLC, Dubai, United Arab Emirates

thedreamworkcollective.com

Printed and bound in the United Arab Emirates
Cover and design: Dania Zafar
Text © Mahra Ali Alali

ISBN: 9789948877844

The content of this book is approved for circulation according to the age classification system issued by the Ministry of Culture and Youth.

MC-02-01-2602103
Age Classification E

BUILD A BETTER YOU

FOR TEENS

How to Become the Best Version of
Yourself in Seven Easy Steps

MAHRA ALI ALALI

To every person who helped me, encouraged me,

and stood by my side while I was writing this book.

To you, the person reading this.

To the person who will change the future.

To the person who will create a better community

for the next generation.

I wish you all the best.

Contents

Introduction

This generation is like no other. This world has changed a lot the past decade, from social media to technology to COVID-19. I understand how hard life can be and how demotivating it can get, but I am here to help you get motivated and develop yourself. I would like to help you create a version of yourself you can be proud of. By the end of this book, I hope that I will have empowered you to become not only a changed individual but a better person willing to embrace life and learn a whole new way of living.

Around December 2020, I used to wake up at eight thirty, and I'd be late for class. When I did join the class online, I would do so from the comfort of my bed—I was not focused, and participation went out the window. After school, I would go through my phone, watch videos on TikTok, scroll through Instagram and Snapchat, and mainly stay in bed. There was no sense of motivation, and procrastination became a way of life for me. I wouldn't even go to sleep until two or three in the morning. I got too comfortable, which is extremely dangerous. As Neale Donald Walsch said, "Life begins at the end of your comfort zone." It's important to never get too comfortable—avoid this at all costs.

This may be your routine right now, and that is okay, but my goal is to inspire you to take control of your life and be intentional with your time. Floyd Mayweather Jr. once said, "You have good days, you have bad days, but the main thing is to grow mentally." It is okay that we all have our bad days if they are because of stress, anxiety, friendship or relationship problems, or family issues; these things are all parts of life. What's important is that we learn from our bad days and take action after these moments have passed.

If you are wondering how I am right now, I wake up at six o'clock, exercise, clean my room, and make myself a good breakfast along with a cup of coffee. Then I get my notes ready for class. After school, I read for thirty minutes and do my homework. Following this, I code, play the piano, entertain myself with a game of chess, and sometimes paint. Eventually, I take a thirty-minute break; fifteen minutes of this time is spent in meditation. The remaining fifteen minutes I spend writing my schedule for the next day (this proactive step is helpful, and I will explain more about this in the chapter titled Way #1). I am asleep by ten o'clock. I can say that I am capable and exceeding what I thought I was limited to being. I got through many hard times and managed to get over my procrastination issues. Now I know my worth and how valuable and special I am; I know how strong I am. I got through a really rough time, and I still have room to grow and get better. I want to help you recover, exceed, excel, become superior to the current version of you, and, above all, make yourself proud of who you are.

This book will help you start a new chapter on a clean blank page (which we all need at some point in life) without having to go through a rough time. The seven ways I provide will help you, inspire you, and get you started. Above all, it's all written clearly in simple English. This book will take you on a journey that will intrigue you and challenge you.

When I was around eleven years old, I remember my mom would always give me very long and boring books to read. I would read the first three pages of one and put it back on the shelf, then never touch it again. Then I found the books that interested me, and I started reading and enjoying them.

I hope you take an interest in this book and don't throw it back on the shelf after the first few pages. It's short, simple, and effective, with the goal of helping develop a better you. If you follow the seven methods I give you, you may become a little uncomfortable as you try to change your old self, develop new habits, and change your lifestyle, but allow this to be the catalyst to becoming the productive person you are meant to be. The seven ways mentioned in this book guided me to become who I am today. Don't be afraid to make mistakes—in fact, make more mistakes, take the risk, know your worth, let go of your past, live your life with purpose, and know it's okay if you still don't know your purpose in life yet. (This book will hopefully get you closer to finding out what you were made for.) It's time to change your mindset, be selfish, take care of yourself before others, and accept the fact that you can't please everyone. There will always be people who are against you. (I will talk about that more with Way #7.)

The sooner you start working on yourself, the better. Remember to take your time while reading and grasp as much information as possible. Do the activities provided in the book and keep a highlighter and notebook to contemplate the things that stand out to you. Rewrite your key takeaways in your own words, summarizing them to internalize what you learned from each chapter. Enjoy this time, and embrace how simple yet effective this book is. I wish you all the best as you change who you are, develop yourself, and start a bright, new chapter of your life.

Mahra Ali

Getting Started

Hello! My name is Mahra Al Ali. At the time of writing this, I am thirteen years old and live in the United Arab Emirates, where I am from. I'm not sure how you got this book, but I am really happy you did. I wish you all the best, and I hope you learn a lot from it. Now all you have to do is keep on reading.

Let's get started. I'll start with this: never say "I am the best version of myself." It's impossible to truly become the best version of yourself because there is always a way to get better. *Always.* You can never be the absolute best version of yourself. As you grow, your limits expand, your expectations increase, you become more capable, and your standards heighten. In short, you will never be able to become the best version of yourself because there will always be a way to become even better. There is always room for improvement, and I would like to help you improve.

Life Centered

Many of us center our lives on a specific thing. For instance, some people center their lives on their grades, their friends, their parents, their hobbies, etc. In general, centering your life on anything is unhelpful, as you should not have one thing controlling your life. Your happiness or your emotions should never be based on pleasing someone or living up to their expectations. Your life is so much more than that.

My uncle once told me "لا تعطين شيء اكبر من حجمه," and this translates to "Do not give something bigger than its size." You may ask what this means. In essence, he was telling me not to care about something more than I should, because I would end up being hurt when the person leaves or the situation changes. For instance, you pour water into a cup and over-fill it. Are you going to get mad at the cup? No. It is your fault for giving it bigger than its size.

Never center your life on getting good grades. That doesn't mean you shouldn't focus on your studies—after all, they are the key to a great future—but remember that you have a life outside of them. If you get a bad mark, it is not going to be the end of the world; you can do better next time.

Another example is your friends. Don't center your life on your friends, and never live to impress them or exceed their expectations. Know that you are your own person: an individual. You should embrace this. Don't let a disagreement or miscommunication with friends ruin your entire week. You have a life outside of the people you hang out with, so it's important that you do not waste a second being upset with people whom you cannot control.

Your life is divided into different facets, and you should never allow one of these parts to hold more importance than it needs to. The most important thing is to be a good person. Having a pleasant personality is what defines you and makes you the person you truly are. Focus on your personality and yourself; make that your priority, as this will stay with you your entire life. All the other aspects of your life have their smaller functions, but your personality (what makes up you) should always remain in the center.

Summary of the 7 Ways to Become a Better You

Way #1: Be Productive and Don't Procrastinate

Have a schedule, write down your goals, avoid distractions, and focus on yourself—be selfish.

Way #2: Make Mistakes and Take Risks

Never be afraid to make mistakes; in fact, make more mistakes, and learn from them.

Way #3: Know Your Worth

Understand how important you are.

Way #4: Let Go

Let go of the past, move on, and don't over-
think it.

Way #5: Live Life with Passion

Give yourself a reason to get out of bed.

Way #6: Change Your Mindset

Look at the world from different views, and never judge people.

Way #7: Be Selfish

Don't do anything that makes you unhappy. Please yourself; gift yourself.

Be Productive and Don't Procrastinate

The moment a person is born, they begin to die. Read that again.

Some people die faster, and others die slower, but none of us get to decide when we die. Let me pose a question to you: What would you do if I told you that you had one week left to live? Would you still do what you are doing every day? If not, change that right now. Every single second in your life counts, whether you are lying in bed doing nothing or you are developing your life's purpose. Make your life count—be productive.

What Is Procrastination?

I was listening to a podcast, and Eric Thomas said he once met a girl from Australia, and she told him she was a procrastinator. He then stopped her and said, "I do not believe in such a thing. If I told you I would give you a million dollars if you came here at five a.m. sharp, would you show up?"

The girl responded, "Of course I would show up. I would be here at four fifty-nine a.m., ready to get that million dollars."

This shows that there is no such thing as procrastination; there are just certain things that do not motivate you. Since these things don't motivate you, you don't make them a priority. Just like the girl: money motivated her to get up in the morning; she wasn't a chronic procrastinator. So what should you do?

If you need something to get done, have a sense of urgency about it; make it your top priority. Find what gets you going daily, and make it your number one priority to keep it always in front of you. When you find out what's important to you, what your purpose is, what motivates you, I promise you will get up early, be the first one to show up, and do whatever it takes to be number one. For example, someone's purpose is to help others develop. That is what motivates them to get things done.

At the end of the day, there is no such thing as procrastination. There is only lack of motivation and priorities.

Let's find out how to gain motivation.

Law of Attraction

Don't worry: I am not here to give you a physics lesson. The law of attraction is simple: you will attract in your life whatever you focus on. Whatever you give your energy and attention to will come to you. For instance, you want a new car—let's say a black Lamborghini Urus. Write down your goal so you are constantly reading it, or put a picture in a place you look at regularly, such as the lock screen on your phone. By doing this, you will attract the car, you will recognize the car more often, and, eventually, you will get the car.

I started practicing this around a year ago, and it does work. I know many people who have done this, and it has worked for them too. Try it, and you will find that the more you talk about something, and the more you see something you want, the more you will attract it into your life. Act as though you are already where you want to be, and the universe will respond. Here are some examples on the law of attraction—doesn't this ever happen to you? You talk about someone, for instance, and they walk through the door minutes after. That is the law of attraction taking action. You attract the person by talking about them. Have you ever learned a new word or phrase and started hearing it on TV or on the radio multiple times? That is also an example of the law of attraction.

Write Your Vision

Listen up! You *have* not because you *ask* not.

What does that mean? You don't have what you want because you didn't ask for it. By this I don't mean go ask your parents or your partner for a new Birkin bag. I mean you didn't ask God or whatever you believe in for what you want.

I dare you to do one simple thing—something basic that anyone can do but only a really small amount of people actually do. Something that will flip your entire world over and change everything. I promise you it will work; trust me on this.

I know many people who have tried it and it worked for them. Steve Harvey does it as well. I dare you to write down one hundred things that you want. Yes, one hundred. You may not have anything more to come up with by the time you reach thirty, but do not stop until you reach one hundred. Think of the future—the house you want, the car you want, your dream body; anything your mind can come up with. Make it as detailed as possible. After you've completed your list, read it every day for a year, and by the end of the year, tick off the things that you've received or accomplished. I promise you that there will be more than ten things marked off.

Doing this exercise attracts the one hundred things you desire. It makes you prioritize your life by reading your desires every day. This will motivate you and make you work toward receiving all that you want. By doing this one step, you are attracting what you want for your life.

Make a Vision Board

Most successful people have a vision board. What is a vision board? A vision board involves putting pictures of the things you want in a place that is constantly in your view—for example, your cabinet or in front of the desk you study at, at work, or maybe on your phone lock screen.

This is just another exercise to do to attract what you want in life. It is a motivational tool to help you work toward achieving your life goals. My vision board had ice skates and a blue iPhone 12 Pro Max, and after about a month, I had both items. My mom does this as well, and she will tell you that it works for her.

Make a Schedule

A simple thing that is totally life-changing is to take five minutes before you go to bed and write your schedule for the next day. This will help you become more productive. Take note not to make your schedule so detailed and tight that you will get bored and feel like a robot. Change it up a bit. Here is an example of my own schedule.

6:30 a.m.—wake up and get ready for school

7:00 a.m.—make coffee, walk outside

7:30 a.m.—eat breakfast

8:00 a.m.—attend school

10:30 a.m.—work out

11:00 a.m.—get back to class

1:00 p.m.—read

1:30 p.m.—eat lunch

2:00 p.m.—take a phone break

2:30 p.m.—do my homework

3:30 p.m.—play chess

4:00 p.m.—play piano

4:30 p.m.—study with siblings

5:00 p.m.—sit outside

5:30 p.m.—listen to motivational podcasts and
draw/paint

6:00 p.m.—write

9:00 p.m.—sit with siblings

10:00 p.m.—meditate

10:30 p.m.—sleep

You can dedicate a notebook you have to creating your daily schedules. It will help you through the day and is truly life changing.

The key is not to prioritize what's on your schedule, but to schedule your priorities.
—STEPHEN COVEY

Make sure what you put on your schedule is a priority.

Surround Yourself with Positive People

Surrounding yourself with positive people will eventually make you positive.

*Show me your friends, and I
will show you your future.*
—DAN PEÑA

*You are the average of the five people
you spend the most time with.*
—JIM RON

It is known that you become like the people
you surround yourself with, whether they are
good or bad, so be discerning about whom
you become friends with. When you surround
yourself with productive, respectful, wise, and
positive people, you will take on those same
traits. The opposite is also true. If you surround
yourself with negative, lazy, rude people, you
will also exhibit those characteristics. Try your
best to surround yourself with people better
than you—people whom you look up to and

whose opinions you value—so you can become a better person. A piece of advice I got from a teacher is "Never take advice from someone you are not willing to switch places with." Always keep that in mind before taking any piece of advice from anyone.

Overthinking

Distractions

None of us can say we don't distract ourselves, as we all have this tendency, including me. What we have to do is learn to not distract ourselves with useless things that waste our time on a daily basis. There are many things that distract us, of course, and here are a couple:

1. Complaining

The word *complain* means to "express grief, pain, or discontent." If you want to stay where you are, complain.

We all complain, and we complain a lot, but truth be told, it's such a waste of time. It's useless and won't help you. Life is not about complaining; it's about living the best way possible.

Complaining won't solve one little thing. There is always this instinct that tells you you've had enough, that you need to rest and take a break. *Never* listen to that instinct! (Keep in mind taking a little break is normal, but never make it a habit.) This is what will make you stand out from other people. While others listen to this complaint of weariness and complacency, you don't have to. This instinct is like a defense mechanism that wants to get you out. When you feel miserable and sad, instead of complaining, you can change your perspective on it.

Let me tell you a story about a boy. He lived with his poor family in a really small house, and he was ashamed of them. One day he went to his friend's house and saw that his friend's parents weren't home, so he asked, "Where are your parents?" His friend responded, "They passed away last summer." The boy felt really sorry for his friend and realized how blessed he was to have a family. Instead of complaining about how poor he was, now he was grateful for having such a loving family. You see, there are always people who aren't as fortunate as us, so we have to be grateful for what we have and not complain.

2. Other People

Many people have one person they simply can't tolerate; however, I believe no one is completely evil, and eventually they will show you their good side.

A mantra that I've taken as my own is "Kill them with kindness," as said by Selena Gomez. As much as other people do wrong by me, I make it a point to always treat them with kindness no matter what.

Here's an example of this:

I once knew this girl—let's call her Rouda—and she was known for her attitude. She was needy and nosy and would never apologize for any of her hurtful actions. I was forced to spend time with her because she was like family. Rouda did many bad things to me, and I mean *many*. She tried bringing me down many times, and every time I found a new friendship, she would do anything to ruin it. She made up rumors about me and made many people believe them. Despite all this, I treated her with respect and kindness. I never did anything bad to her in return, and though I would be annoyed, I still would never have mistreated her. Even now, I have never told any of her secrets to anyone.

Roudah once did something that hurt me. When I found out, I was furious. Despite this, I still treated her with respect and kindness.

She recognized that I never stopped treating her nicely, even though she was so mean to me. I believe it is because I never changed my attitude toward her that she eventually came to me and apologized. A person who never apologizes told me that what she had done was wrong.

This proves my point: no one is pure evil, and everyone has a soft spot—just give them time. If anyone does something to hurt you, you have to let it go and lead yourself down the right path. Karma will take care of it. (I will talk more about this in Way #4.)

What Can You Control?

We drain our energy and worry about things we can't control instead of doing what we can. We should shift all our energy into things we can control.

You cannot control how you look. You can't control who your family is. You can't control what happens in your life or how others treat you. We can't control our pasts; however, we can control our responses to life's circumstances.

In summary, those things that cannot be changed won't change. Continually thinking about them only causes anxiety. What you can control is what you focus on. Why waste your time complaining about something you can't control when you can spend your time changing what you *can* control?

Keep Yourself Busy

Try your best to keep yourself busy. Do the things that interest you. Join courses, try new things, and find something that intrigues you and makes you happy. This will help you in many different ways. It will help you find your purpose and your *why*. (I'll talk more about that in Way #5.)

Saying No

A quality of every successful person is the courage to say no when they need to say no. It takes discipline to stay on the path that leads them to their greatest self, even if it means losing people and leaving things behind.

Saying no to things that you know will ruin your future and waste your time and energy is really important. For example, your friend may take up smoking in high school. You will feel left out by saying no, but you also know it's bad for your health. Taking up a smoking habit will add no value to your future, and you are wasting your time and energy by doing it. So you have to say "*No!*"

Don't ever be afraid to say no. Let's say you are stressed with work or school, and one of your friends wants you to help them out with a project. You may feel bad, but you already have too much work of your own that you must focus on. Never be afraid to say no, and if they are really your friend, they will understand. Saying no does not make you bad. On the contrary, it makes you a better person. It shows that you are putting yourself first and not others. You must prioritize yourself.

You've heard people say "Love yourself," "Help yourself first," or "Prioritize yourself," as you are your main character, and no one is in control of your life but you. The more times you say no with clarity and purpose, the more freedom you will have in the future.

It may be hard, and it may hurt, but saying no to those things that don't serve your purpose is powerful. Don't be afraid! Say no!

Read, Read, Read

Do you know how important reading is? It is the thing that transformed me and made me who I am. It changed my point of view on life and has expanded my world. Reading changes your personality and broadens your horizons. There are many benefits to reading, such as:

1. Reducing stress

2. Increasing vocabulary and comprehension

3. Helping develop empathy

4. Improving brain connectivity

My uncle was on a TV interview once, and he was talking about me. He spoke about my love of reading and how this reading had made me a good listener at a young age. It had also given me insight into perspectives I might not have learned about otherwise and broadened my own worldview, he said that I have knowledge that makes me unique, and that this is all due to my love of reading.

Small Steps to Development

1. Write down your most important goals of the year.

2. Make a vision board of the things you want.

3. Make a schedule for the things you will do tomorrow.

4. Say no to someone this week if you are under a lot of pressure.

5. Read at least thirty pages this week.

6. Stop complaining about something, and be grateful instead.

7. Take time today to sit by yourself and understand yourself.

8. Distance yourself from all the negative people in your life by the end of the week.

Make Mistakes and Take Risks

How risky is life? It's risky to the point where you will never get out alive. I mean *never*—so why not take that risk? Why not go on that once-in-a-lifetime trip? Why not quit that job you hate? Why not start that business everyone told you would fail? Why not go pursue your dream and leave everything else behind? Why not try that sport you always wanted to play?

Why not?

At the end of the day, none of us are getting out alive, so take that risk. The greatest risk of all is not taking one; keep that in mind. When you get over the fear of death, nothing in life can threaten you. You have to be willing to give it all up.

If someone told you that you had one week to live, would you have any regrets? Would you regret not spending enough time with your family or not going on that dream trip? Steve Jobs would ask himself these types of questions every single day, and if the answer was no a couple of days in a row, he would know that he was doing something wrong and that something had to change.

Take More Risks

The person who risks nothing has nothing, does nothing, and is nothing. Many people are scared to lose, to make mistakes, to fail. There is no reason to fear.

As a child I had this bracelet—actually, I still do. It has *I never lose—I either win or learn* written on it. I live by that, and it means a lot to me as a chess player. I would wear that bracelet at every chess tournament I played, and before each game, I would tell myself, *Mahra, do your best, and try to win, but remember—you are not here to win but to learn, so it's okay. You aren't losing; you're learning. Good luck!* I'd say a little prayer after that and start the game.

I used to try my best not to feel sad when I lost. Instead, I would figure out my mistake and not repeat it. My dad used to tell me, "It's okay to make mistakes. What's not okay is to repeat them." Never be afraid to make mistakes or to fail. Jack Ma Yun once said, "If you succeed, every mistake becomes legendary."

Be willing to fail. Get used to the fact that you will fail. You will never know if you sink or float unless you jump into the water, so take the risk; only a person who risks is free.

Fail More

Keep on failing and failing. Failing is better than never trying.

One thing you should never do, and I mean *never*, is blame others for your failures. A person who blames others for their failure will never be successful. You are the one in control of your life. Never blame a single soul for something in your life that is your fault—just fix it. But always be willing to fail.

I heard a story of a boy and his sister, Sara Blakely (who is an American businesswoman, entrepreneur, and founder of Spanx). They lived with their father, and when they were children, their father would teach them and encourage them to fail at something every week. He would ask them at the dinner table what they failed at that week, and if they had no answer, he would get disappointed. The children would think of what they had done wrong that week and felt that pressure to try something new in order to fail.

Sara came back from school and reported, "Dad! Dad! I tried out for the soccer team, and I was horrible!"

Her dad high-fived her and responded, "Way to go! Good job, sweetheart!"

How strange. What a unique way of parenting. Many parents would encourage their kids to succeed and make them believe that failure is bad, that they should get away from such a concept. The father in the story made his kids understand that it is okay to make mistakes and that it is not bad. He also taught them that they should not repeat their mistakes. This will help his children in the future and make them understand that failing is normal and that it's okay. It instils in the child that it is not okay to never try.

If we never fail, we will never change our strategies. Everything would always work out because we would never take a risk. The point of failing is to rise and work toward our purpose, doing what's right and fixing what we did wrong without blaming anyone but ourselves.

Don't Expect It to Be Easy

Easy should never be in your vocabulary. If you want an easy life, be average, avoid all new ventures, take no risks, avoid all things that are even the tiniest bit daunting.

Do you want a normal life with no purpose but to work, or do you want to be remembered as someone who made a difference? If you want to make a difference, you might lose everything. You may have people against you, even those closest to you. You may have many bad days; in fact, you *will* have more bad days than good. Don't worry—this is normal. You will learn more from your bad days than the good ones. You will feel like giving up, and you will get fed up; however, in order to be successful, you have to move forward. Every time you fall, it's imperative that you get back up. This road won't get any easier—just keep working hard.

I have had so many bad days. In fact, I had a bad day yesterday, and despite that, I am here, writing about life not being easy. In order to make a difference, you have to outsmart and outwork everyone around you. Wake up earlier than everyone. If everyone wakes up at eight, you should wake up at six, or go to sleep later than everyone; whatever suites you. *Mahra, what am I supposed to do in those extra hours?* Take advantage of them: meditate, work out, study, do all your extra work. Not everyone cares about their marks or their futures. Everyone takes days off when they feel like it, but you

are not everyone else, and you keep working.
You choose your future.

In order for a glow stick to glow, you have to
break it. In order to get a rainbow, you have
to put up with the rain. Life may break you,
and there may be rain, but this is part of the
process to success. Trust the process.

Happiness

No matter who you are and how much money
you make, you will have bad days. There will
be days that you feel unhappy.

Happiness is misunderstood by many people. Happiness is not something you maintain your entire life; you have to work to keep it.

What is something that everyone deserves but very few people enjoy? Happiness. Some people are not happy, although they have all they need in life—a wonderful family, a good job, and a big house! They are good people too, yet they are not happy. Why?

Ben Carson said, "Happiness does not result from what we get but what we give."

As students, teachers, parents, and many others that shape our lives, we have a civil responsibility to improve our personal development in order to discharge our social responsibility. However, not everyone feels true happiness! Some people are not happy because they don't have money or a job; their circumstances are not the best. But do these things define what we need to be happy? I don't think so!

You don't have to *have* something in order to be happy. In fact, I believe in order to be happy, you must be a giver. Some people don't have a good job or even a family, and yet they are so giving. If you ask them if they are happy, they would most likely say yes! Hosea Ballou once said, "Real happiness is cheap enough, yet how dearly we pay for its counterfeit." Real happiness is so cheap, but we pay so much for the fake one. You don't really need the new iPhone or the designer bag to be happy. Giving is the key to true happiness.

Everyone wants to be something, thinking this will make them happy. Some want to have a degree, while others want to lose weight. I believe that accepting ourselves for who we are and others for who they are sparks great happiness that can be enjoyed instantly!

How can someone be happy while judging everyone around them? We have to be tolerant and accept those around us. Tolerance is important—without it, the world will be a hateful and negative place. Sheikh Zayed (may God have mercy upon him) once said, "A good believer should be merciful and tolerant; only the hard hearted can be ruthless." The higher our tolerance level, the happier we will be.

Do you think anyone in this world has been happy all their life? Of course not! Happiness is not something we can maintain all our lives, and it comes and goes just like the waves! And this is okay! You don't believe me? Well, Lionel Messi was loved and supported by his poor but loving family. He was happy! Then his beloved grandmother passed away. He was so close to her. He fell into a deep depression and felt as though his life were falling apart. He even stopped playing soccer for some time. Then he thought of his grandmother and wanted her to be proud of him, so he began playing again.

While playing, he was diagnosed with a growth hormone deficiency, which meant that he couldn't physically grow like other children. His parents could not afford the medical treatment, and his soccer club refused to pay for it. Other clubs spotted his talent but did not want him to join because of his condition. Life went on, and he lost all his hopes of becoming a professional soccer player. Until Barcelona spotted him and offered to cover his treatment! Look at him now! He is one of the highest-paid soccer players in the world!

You see, happiness comes and goes, but you have to work for it and never lose faith.

A word of warning: happiness is not something

you work for once and get for life! You have to keep working for it the rest of your life. In fact, one has to find happiness in the journey and not the destination. Don't expect to feel happy forever after giving to others only once. Don't expect to feel happy forever after being tolerant toward others once. Happiness comes with the consistent act of kindness.

Two years or so ago, I was in Japan riding the bullet train from Tokyo to Osaka. It took two to three hours. I looked out the window, and I noticed this thick black line beneath the train. It caught my attention. It is supposed to support the train but kept disappearing and coming back and disappearing and coming back again! When it disappeared, the train kept on moving normally. It didn't collapse; it didn't have to stop or even slow down. I was curious, and I thought for some time. I told myself that black line was just like happiness. Happiness would come and go, and it is normal. Just like the train, you will not collapse or stop; you have to move on and keep going forward. Never stop and look back. Again, it is the journey!

Fear

Fear is false evidence appearing real. Being afraid of something that has not happened and may never happen is due to beliefs, past thoughts, and conditions.

Fear either means:

Forget

Everything

And

Run

or

Face

Everything

And

Rise

The choice is yours.

Instead of letting your fear control you and stop you from moving forward, allow it to motivate you and drive you. Let fear be your signal to go and not to stop. Face your fear, and let it push you to take that risk, to do what you're afraid of. If you fear public speaking, go speak in public. If you have a fear of heights, go to the tallest building in the world. If you have a fear of starting a business and losing your money, take that risk and open that business. If you have a fear of losing, lose more. If you have a fear of making mistakes, make more. Give yourself that power. There are two types of people in this world: the ones who are consumed by their fears and those who live through their fears.

What is the number one reason people don't

live their dreams? It's not the lack of money, and it's not luck—it's never luck. It is fear. Fear is the greatest killer of dreams; it is that voice inside you that says, "You can't. You're not good enough." It gets louder and louder the more you listen. Fear is the voice of average people, the voice of settlers. You must kill your greatest fear. Never give up until you kill your greatest fear. Get all the courage to go face that fear. Whatever you fear right now, get up and go do it. Your largest fear carries your greatest growth.

Guess what my fear was? It was losing that one person who meant the world to me, and I don't mean in terms of them passing away— that is not in my hands. I mean losing them as in them leaving me. I would do anything for them to stay, and I used to tell them they were right when I knew they were wrong. I would treat them like royalty just so I wouldn't lose them. Now I don't have them. I lost them, and when they left, I politely held the door open for them. I am not telling you it was easy. It was hell, but thank God I got through it and learned the most from that experience. A nice piece of advice: people are going to come into and leave your life. If they want to come in, leave the door open, and if they want to leave, the door is also open. Never beg anyone to stay. If they want to leave, let them go, and wish them the greatest journey. Life will be okay without them. Also know that it is okay to kick people out. It is your life, after all. Letting them go will make you feel lighter. It empowers you; you won't feel like you have to be perfect to keep them around. Keep this in mind, though: not all friendships are bad for you, and sometimes they're worth fighting for. I'll write more about this in Way #5.

Let's get back to our topic of fear. The feeling you have after you've faced your fear and learn from it is indescribable.

Small Steps to Development

1. What did you fail at this week?

2. Today, go do one thing you were afraid to do before.

3. Try to make someone happy today by doing something simple.

4. Take a risk this week at anything.

5. Try something new, even if you may fail at it.

6. Teach someone something you learned from this chapter.

Know Your Worth

Have you ever felt like you've lost your value? Have you felt worthless and of no use, as though one mistake has ruined your entire life? I was watching a speech and the speaker shared this with the audience, and I fell in love with his words. Take this into consideration: You have this one-dollar bill. You ball up the dollar bill. Is it still worth one dollar? Maybe it's now worth only ninety cents because it's crumpled up, right? No! It's still worth one dollar. Then you step on that dollar bill. Is it still worth one dollar? It might have dropped to eighty cents by now. *No!* It is still worth one dollar. Then you spill coffee all over it. Now it must be around seventy cents. Nope, it's still worth one dollar. Then you rip it in half. Is it still worth one dollar? Surely it's only sixty cents by now. That bill is still one dollar—you can tape it back together. So, wait—I squished it, stepped on it, spilled coffee all over it, and then ripped it in half, and you're telling me that I can pick that dollar up, wipe it, and tape it back together, and it is still worth one dollar? If this dollar bill did not lose its value, why do you feel like you have?

No matter what you have been through— stepped on, ripped apart, or hurt—I am here to tell you that you are still you and have not lost your worth. You will never lose your worth, even if you are going through a hard time and are experiencing heartache. You still have value, and there is nothing anyone can do about it.

You can increase your worth only when you add another nine dollars to that dollar bill. Now you are worth ten dollars. No one can tell you how much you are worth; this is a decision for you to make. Don't let anyone put a price on you. Set your own price, and don't give discounts by trying to be like others.

I'm Too Good for Everyone

A wise man once told me to be a very expensive

jewel, as not anyone can see that expensive jewel or buy it, and an expensive jewel is locked away in a glass box and is only touched gently with gloves on. On the other hand, a normal jewel can be touched, bought, and seen by everyone. He told me this to show me that I have to see how unique I am. I must know that I deserve to be handled with care, that I am worth too much to let anyone put a price on me.

It is not a bad thing to have this sort of mentality. In fact, it is a very good thing. This is knowing your value or worth so no one can play with your feelings, improperly touch you, or get too close, because you are precious and unique. This does not mean you are disrespectful or count others as worthless. Your speech should always be filled with grace and knowledge, but make it a point to never lower your value and worth for people who do not deserve you or your time.

Places that Value You

I'll tell you a very famous and effective story about a father and his son.

A father, before he died, said to his son:

"This is a watch your grandfather gave me. It is more than two hundred years old, but before I give it to you, go to the watch shop on the street, and tell him I want to sell it, and see how much it is worth."

The son went to the watch shop and then came back to his father and told him, "The watchmaker said he'll pay five dollars because it's too old."

The father said, "Go to the jewelry store."

The son went to the jewelry store and then came back to his father and said, "They offered me one hundred dollars because it's scratched."

The father said, "Go to the museum, and show them the watch."

The son questioned his father but did it anyway and went to the museum. He came back and said to his father, "They offered me a million dollars for this rare piece to be included in their antique collection."

The father said, "I wanted to show you that the right place will value you in the right way. Don't put yourself in the wrong place and get angry if they don't value you. Those who know your value are those who appreciate you. Never stay in a place where someone doesn't see your value or where you don't feel appreciated."

Being in a place where you are valued is extremely important. This will affect your life in many ways, making you a better person mentally and physically. It is part of living a happy life.

People Will Let You Down

My uncle always says, to the point there my family gets fed up, "الشجرة المثمرة هي التي ترمى بالأحجار," which specifically translates to: "The tree with fruit is the one that is thrown at with stones." This means that the tree with value and fruit is the tree that people normally pick on—the tree that most people throw rocks at.

What does this have to do with knowing your worth? People don't pick on just anyone. People pick on the person with fruit or the person with value and standards. When people pick on you or try to bring you down, know that it means you're valuable and special. They left all of the world's worries and concerns to try to bring you down. Count it as a joy that you are special, and feel sorry for them. They must be going through a lot themselves and are taking out their insecurities on others. Remember Selena Gomez's words: kill them with kindness. No matter what anyone does to you, treat them with kindness, and stand tall no matter how hard they try to bring you down.

Consider the following example from my friend Maria's experience:

My name is Maria, I am fourteen years old, and I would like to share something that happened to me. There are these two girls—let's call them Alissa and Abby. Neither of them liked me for no particular reason. I was really close to them, and they were my family, but they did not like me. They would go and ruin my friendships with everyone I got close to. For instance, they once went to my friend, whom I was on good terms with, and told her that I gossiped about her, that I did not like her, and a bunch of bad things about me that were not true.

How did I respond?

I kept silent and treated them in the best way possible. I was hurt inside but did not let anyone know. They kept on hurting me, and I kept treating them back with kindness and respect. Then Alissa and Abby came up to me and asked why I didn't get mad or treat them badly back. I responded, "Treating you badly will only lower my standards. I never treat anyone badly in the hopes that they learn from me." They were shocked with my response and apologized, as they had not meant to hurt me.

You see, you should cut off harmful friendships while still being respectful and kind. You should extend grace to those who hurt you and not put yourself in an environment where you will continue to be hurt. You will be happy that way, as you don't put your thoughts and energy into their negativity. Live your life, and treat everyone the best way possible.

How Do You See Yourself?

When you are all alone, who do you see? Do you see an independent, valuable person who can change the world, or do you see an average person who has nothing to offer, living with no purpose?

Only you can tell what you see. Will you undersell yourself, or will you show the world your value?

No one will come up to you and tell you that you are worth more than you think you are. This is something you must realize on your own.

How do I raise my value? What am I worth? These are questions only you can answer. It is your own self-worth, and you get to decide how high or low it is. How do you think of yourself when you are alone with no one around you? That is your self-worth. You raise your self-worth by deciding that you are worth more. Really easy, right? It is a decision only you have to make.

The people who you have to get rid of in your life are the people who question your worth. If they don't value you, then they don't deserve you.

Love Yourself

Self-love has nothing to do with money, cars, jobs, or anything materialistic. Loving yourself is about knowing your self-worth. It is knowing that you don't need to please others and instead focusing on pleasing yourself. People pleasers never end up happy because they center their lives on making others happy, forgetting about themselves.

Love yourself, believe in yourself, know your worth. Self-love is the only cure to self-hate. After loving yourself, you will never need anyone else. A majority of the people in your life are temporary; only a small percent of the people you know will stay with you for a long time. You are the only person who will stay with yourself *forever*, no matter what.

If you don't love yourself, find out why, and change it. Make your future self proud. When people ask me who I look up to, I immediately respond, "I look up to the future me. The me in ten years—that's who I look up to." When they ask me again in ten years, I will respond with the exact same answer. People may think it's strange and that I'm crazy, but think about it: if I look up to the future me, the future me will look up to the future them. It is confusing—I am aware of that—but let that sink in for a minute.

Do what makes you happy; follow what allows you to love yourself. As long as you aren't hurting anyone, continue to be you.

Another important quality is not judging others. A new girl came to class. She was social and made friends easily. One of my classmates went up to her and asked her how she managed to make friends so quickly.

She responded, "The secret to making friends is simple—don't judge anyone. Just let them be."

I learned a lot from that, and I stopped being critical of others. Because of this, many of my friends trusted me more. Furthermore, strangers would share their stories with me, knowing I would not judge them.

Treating people the way you want to be treated is the key to self-love. Be happy for others so others will be happy for you, and even if they aren't, there is no point in being negative.

I love myself too much to allow myself to sit with negative people or those who cannot applaud the success of others. Negative and envious individuals will destroy you and will take away all your self-love.

People will try to rip you apart, but know your worth. Love yourself to the point that you don't care who they are. If someone is standing in the way of your success, they aren't worth your energy, even if they are family. Those who love you will stand by you, not against you. Also be wise and careful about who you share your value with. Love yourself to the point that you don't get offended or hurt by anyone besides yourself.

Small Steps to Development

1. Leave any place you are not valued.

2. Spend time alone.

3. Change the negative ways you see yourself.

4. Tell yourself that you love yourself.

5. Write a letter to the future you, and open it on your birthday.

6. Try not to judge anyone.

Let Go

Sometimes holding on does more damage than letting go. Many things are going to happen to you during your lifetime. You will be hurt, taken advantage of, and left, and the best thing you can do about it all is to let go and move on. Sometimes you hold on to unnecessary things that are weighing you down, so you have to let go of them in order to rise.

Why is letting go hard? It's because of attachments, and attachments = suffering. To make it more clear unhealthy attachments = suffering. How do I know the difference between a healthy and an unhealthy attachment? An unhealthy friendship/relationship will include jealousy, deflecting responsibility, and blame. Essentially, unhealthy attachments make you not yourself. We are prone to base our happiness and lives on people or things, or both, that we should not attach ourselves to, causing us pain. Yet when we let go, we make space for better things to enter our lives.

Most people find it hard to let go of the following:

1. Emotions

How can a person possibly let go of their emotions? Does it mean they become numb? Of course not! Letting go of your emotions helps you not take things so seriously or react harshly.

My teacher once told me a story about a snake and a saw. The snake went into a room, and as it moved around, it hit the handsaw and thought it was a threat to him. The snake immediately bit the saw, which cut the snake's mouth. The snake then wrapped itself around the saw, thinking it could suffocate the saw. This did nothing to the saw; however, the snake was killed by the sharp blades on its supposed enemy. The snake was killed by its own anger and reaction to something it thought was a threat.

You see, many of us are the same as the snake—we react to situations in life that we think will harm us, and it causes us to hurt ourselves. This mentality also hurts us. Holding on to all the negative emotions and thoughts makes us suffer. When we react in anger, it makes those around us suffer.

It is best to ignore negative emotions and let go of pessimistic thoughts toward anyone or anything. Instead of reacting angrily when someone does something wrong to us, we should try to understand the person and where they are coming from and show compassion. Holding on does nothing good to our future; we must let go. We have to move on before our emotions consume us and ruin our lives like the snake with the saw. Don't hold on—instead, move on, and focus on creating the best life for yourself.

2. The Past

"Yesterday is history, tomorrow is a mystery, today is a gift—that's why they call it the present." This is one of my favorite quotes from Eleanor Roosevelt.

I believe that one of the hardest things to do is let go of the past. Remember your past doesn't define you. You are not your past. Timon from *The Lion King* said, "You gotta put your past behind you." Rafiki also pointed out, "The past can hurt, but the way I see it, you can either run from it or learn from it." The past can hurt you a lot, but remember that you can't change what happened in the past. With time, you will get over everything that happened to you.

I'd like to share a story I read online about two traveling monks who reached a river where they met a young woman waiting to cross.

Scared of the current, the young woman asked one of the monks if he could carry her across.

The monk hesitated, but the other one quickly picked her up and put her on his shoulders, transported her across the water, and put her down on the other bank.

She thanked him and then departed.

As the monks continued on their journey, the other monk became obsessed and preoccupied with his own thoughts. Unable to hold his silence any longer, he spoke out.

"Brother, our spiritual training teaches us to avoid any and all contact with women, but you picked that young woman up and put her onto your shoulders, then carried her across the river, breaking this most sacred rule."

"Brother," the first monk calmly replied, "this happened many, many miles back. It was *I* who carried the young woman, and it was *I* who placed her down on the other side over an hour ago. So why, brother, are *you* still carrying her?"

We all can become obsessed with thoughts running around in our minds. Letting go is easy to say but can seem so difficult to do. Mastering this vital skill for happiness requires practice and training of the mind. Like in the story, we need to let go of the past. It happened, it's over, and it cannot be changed. We must focus on the present.

Hanging on to the past will make you suffer. If you don't leave your past in the past, it can destroy you. Live for what today has to offer, not what yesterday took away. Don't lock yourself in a prison of your past, and quit living in there—let it go.

3. Other People

Losing people is part of the process of letting go. Just trust the process. The process is necessary; don't trip over it.

Some people bring value and joy into your life during certain seasons, but this doesn't mean they are supposed to stay in your life for all seasons. Cherish the good times you had with them, but letting go will enable you to find new relationships for this new season of life. As Thomas Wilder once said, "It's hard to turn the page when you know someone won't be in the next chapter, but the story must go on." Learn to be alone. One thing I repeat to myself is that I am the only person who will stay with me my entire life. This helps me realize that only a small percent of the people in my life are the most valuable assets to keep close. Recognize that anyone who wants to walk out of your life is always free to go—open the door for them, and allow them to walk them out.

As Madea (played by Tyler Perry) once said, there are three types of people in the world: The leaves are seasonal, and when the wind blows, they fly away. They're unstable, and when the season changes, they die and are gone. Most people in the world are like leaves; they take from the tree and give shade. This is all they do.

The branches are the worst, because they will fool you. They look like they are strong, but eventually they will break off.

Finally, if you find a couple people who are the roots, you are most blessed. The roots at the bottom of the tree hold the tree in place and never leave the tree. When you get people in your life who are roots, hold on to them. Let everyone else go.

Be careful who you're friends with. If they won't make you better, they are wasting your time. Learn to be alone and work on loving you.

Some may ask God why they have to let go and

why this part of the process hurts so much. Be encouraged in knowing you are not the only one. We are on this journey together. Here is my friend Anna's experience on letting go:

Hey, my name is Anna. I am seventeen years old, and I would like to share my story. I am not a really social person, but when I talk to someone for a period of time, I get really attached. I had this best friend—let's call her Holly. She and I were extremely close and shared all our secrets; she was like my older sister. We FaceTimed every day before bed. We took care of each other, helped each other, and gave each other advice. She knew everything I was doing twenty-four seven and I knew everything she was doing. Then she started drifting away as she found other friends.

This hurt me to the point that I lost myself. I stopped taking care of myself and lost interest in my hobbies. I just lay in bed all day and went through our photos and read our chats. I didn't understand why Holly would do anything like this to me. Then I accepted the fact that I was holding on to Holly. This was hurting me and weighing me down more than if I simply let go.

I had to move on. I realized that I was not the one missing out on anything. I was a true friend who cared, so it was her who *was losing out. I found better friends and focused on myself more than anyone else, and this helped me a lot.*

We can learn a lot from Anna's story. When we attach ourselves to a person, we can be weighed down and stop living our lives.

4. Yourself

You have to learn to let go of yourself.

What? How do I let go of myself?

Sometimes you feel the pressure to be this person for others and think you can't change who you are. You've put on a facade for others, and now you need to be your true self. You can change who you are and not care what others think.

Do what makes you happy and what makes you comfortable. Let go of the old you—the you who cared about what everyone thought.

Charles Horton Cooley wrote, "I am not what I think I am. I am not what you think I am. I am what I think you think I am."

Let that sink in for a minute. Our identity, or who we are, is based on what others think of us. Or you can say what we think others think of us. For instance, your friend likes this new gorgeous bag; you find yourself buying a similar bag just to impress one person. Living to impress others is unhealthy. Let go of that. Let go of your old habits, and turn your life around. Start fresh and new.

We lie to ourselves when we believe that we are the image we think society will accept. *How do I know who I really am?* Let go of who you are now, and pursue everything that you've ever wanted to do. Don't do anything to please anyone or to fit in. Be different. As Dr. Seuss once said, "Why fit in when you were born to stand out?"

The Importance
of Letting Go

Choosing not to let go of attachments and emotional baggage can be fatal. It's vitally important that you learn to let go. Let's look at the following story I read online about a bird.

Once there was a free bird. She floated in the sky, caught worms for lunch, swam in the summer, and lived a typical bird life. However, she had a habit that every time an event occurred in her life, good or bad, she would pick up a stone from the ground. She sorted out her stones, laughing as she remembered joyful events and crying as she remembered the sad ones.

The bird always took the stones with her, whether she was flying in the sky or walking on the earth—she never let go of them. The years passed, and the free bird collected many stones, but she still kept on sorting through them, remembering the past. It became more and more difficult to fly, and one day the bird was unable to. The bird that had been free some time ago could no longer walk on the earth; she was unable to make a move on her own. She could not catch midges anymore. The bird bravely endured all the hardships and guarded her precious memories. After some time, *the bird died of starvation and thirst with only a pitiful bunch of worthless stones reminding her of her past.*

You see, sometimes you need to let go to grow and move on. Live life to the fullest, and don't let anyone or anything hold you back. Become an unstoppable bird that has nothing holding it back.

5. Never Give Up; It's Part of the Process

I don't care how dark it is, I don't care how much it hurts, I don't care what they said to you or what they said about you—it is not over. No matter what happens to you, it is not over. No matter what you have been through, you're still here and have a great life in front of you.

Remember that it's in front of you, not behind you.

Everyone says "never give up" like it's easy, yet sometimes it's hard and you've had enough. Others tell you to let go like it's the easiest thing you can do and like it can be done in minutes, but letting go is going to be hard at times. It will burn inside, but trust the process, as it will get better. You will feel happy and fulfilled sooner or later.

Everyone wants to make it. It's okay to be sad, it's okay to feel down, it's okay to have a bad day, and it's okay to have an off day. What's not okay is giving up.

Everyone wants to be successful and to experience a miracle, but few are willing to pay the price or deal with problems. The difference between two kinds of ambitious people is that one takes the first step while the other keeps dreaming without doing anything.

This is a story about three birds:

There were three birds on the tree. One bird said it would fly. How many birds were on the tree now? Two? No! There were still three birds on the tree. The bird only said it would fly, but it never did.

What can you learn from this? Sometimes we plan to do things but never do them. We stay in the same place as the people who never planned.

For instance, you planned to go to the gym and take care of yourself but never did it. There is another person who never thought of going to the gym—now both of you are in the same place, even though you planned on going. Everyone wants it, but few are willing to go through the process.

Beautiful things can come from broken pieces if you give the broken pieces a chance. Did you know that butterflies can't see their wings? They can't see how beautiful they are. Most

people are like butterflies—they can't see the
beauty others see in them. Things are going to
happen to you, and people are going to hurt
you, but the best thing you can do is let go
and grow.

Small Steps to Development

1. Let go of something you've been hold-
    ing on to for a long time.

2. Try helping someone let go of another
    person.

3. Never give up, no matter how hard it
    gets. There is always light at the end
    of the tunnel.

4. Be gentle with yourself.

5. Write down your feelings—good or
    bad.

6. Talk to someone about how you
    feel. If you have no one to talk to, try

www.7cups.com, a free online mental health support network with listeners and licensed professionals ready to hear you out.

Live Life with Passion

Why are you here? What is your purpose? What do you want to do with your life? Money is not an answer—think deeper. As Simon Sinek said, everyone knows what they do, and some people know how they do it, but only a few people know why they do it. If you want to live a life of happiness, a life of success, you have to find your purpose.

What gets you out of bed in the morning? It is okay not to know your *why*, but you have to work on finding it. My mom once told me that everyone on this planet is here to do something and has a purpose, and our mission is to go find out what our purpose in life is.

I once heard someone say that when we die, our date of birth gets written on the left side and our day of death on the right, and the dash is in the middle. This determines our timeline on Earth. Within this line are time frames where we were able to impact others and the footprint we left behind to be remembered by. It marks the time during which we built a legacy no one could change. We live in that dash! Some of us have longer dashes, and others have shorter ones, but that does not matter; what matters is what we do within that dash. That dash represents our why.

You get to decide what you do within that dash. This time can be useless and without meaning, or it can be remembered, full of purpose and meaning, making a lasting impact on the world.

Some people will walk this planet and leave it like they were never here, never making an impact or a difference. This is my biggest fear— to have a normal life, a life consumed by work, living without purpose, making no significant change to the world. Simply leaving as if I were never here.

I want to share a story I've heard a couple times about a guy named Average. He lives an average live, in an average school, went to an average university, married an average woman, had average children, with an average job and an average car, living in an average house. He got old and died an average death. Do you know Average? Average is 99 percent of the world's population. You can either be one of those 99 percent or that one percent. The choice is yours. That's the life of a person with no passion or purpose.

If you don't know what drives you or what your purpose is, there is no reason to improve your life. Your purpose has to light a fire inside you. Not knowing your purpose yet is fine.

I once asked my mom what her purpose was, and she replied, "I don't know. My purpose always changes." This puzzled me. How can your purpose possibly change? It's your purpose, after all. Then I realized that you could have more than one purpose and that it's okay for your purpose to change.

For example, someone's purpose was to raise their children to become successful adults. Their purpose would change once those children were older and left—that is okay. You have to look for your purpose in all stages of your life.

How would you feel if you found out you were living someone else's purpose your entire life?

This is why you have to take your time.

How to Find Your Why

Your *why* has to do with four different things: talent, values, passion, and skills. Ask yourself these four questions:

1. What makes you come alive? *Inspire* means "to breathe life into" in Latin. In other words, when you work toward something that inspires you and makes you more alive, you are living in your purpose. When I say "come alive," I am referring to your passion, your *why*.

What inspires you? What makes you alive? What do you like doing? What makes you happy? If you still don't know, it's okay. Ask a friend or a family member you are close to what they think you are good at. When do they see you happy, or what do you do that they think makes you happy? Sit with yourself and find things out about yourself. Talk to yourself as if you're talking to another person. I know this sounds crazy, but try it anyway—you won't regret it!

2. What are your natural strengths? Don't you sometimes wonder why others find certain things hard to do when you can do them easily?

That shows your natural talents.
For instance, I have a flexible back.
Others find things hard to do when
I can do them like they are a piece
of cake. Some people can do a back
bend easily when others can't. That's
their natural talent.

Sometimes "hard work beats talent
when talent doesn't work hard." That's
a quote on my cousin Hour's home
screen on her iPad. I didn't understand
it at first, but then she explained it to
me. She said that if your talent doesn't
work hard, your hard work can beat it.
I interpret it as you don't necessarily
need talent to be successful; working
hard is enough on its own.

Knowing your talent is important, as you can develop it and become better. You can definitely be passionate about things you have no natural talent for. It has been shown that people are normally interested in things they are not naturally talented at. Howard Thurman once wrote, "Don't ask yourself what the world needs; ask yourself what makes you come alive, then go do that. Because what the world needs is people who have come alive."

3. Where do you add the greatest value? In other words: What is important to you? What makes you thrive and work hard? What makes you happy? What do you find

interesting? Look for that, focus on the simplest detail, and ask a friend or anyone close to you where they see you putting a lot of effort in. That will help you find your passion.

4. How will you measure your life? People who don't stand for some-thing can fall for anything. Deciding how you want to measure your life means taking a stand for something or finding the way you want to live and then living your life in that direction. Setting goals and achieve-ments will help you measure your life. One thing you must do is make a list and set yearly goals. Do your best to tick off all your goals by the end of the year.

Outrun Them and Outthink Them

This is a remarkable story of a lion and a gazelle:

Every single morning in Africa, a gazelle wakes up. He has only one thought on his mind and one purpose: to outrun the fastest lion. If he doesn't, he will then be killed and eaten.

Every single morning in Africa, a lion wakes up. He has only one thought on his mind and one purpose: to be able to outrun the slowest gazelle. If he doesn't, he will die of hunger.

Whether you are a gazelle or a lion, there is

one thing you have to do when the sun rises: you must outrun something, whether it is your competition, depression, alcohol, or even your past. You must run faster than you did yesterday, or you will die. You see, even if you are a lion, the king of the jungle with all the power, at the end of the day, you have to work hard to get what you want. You have to work harder and smarter than all your competitors in order to stand out. You may have to wake up two hours before everyone or sleep less and work more. "Sleep faster," as Arnold Schwarzenegger said. Do you think an A+ student puts in the same effort as a D+ student? Of course not. In order to achieve your goals or to become world's best, you must outrun and outwork everyone else.

It Won't Be Easy

Did you know that the root of the word *passion* is *suffering*? Don't expect it to be easy. Don't be average. If you want easy, get an average job, live an average life. Everyone has a dream, but few are willing to pay the price. Here is a story about not giving up when things get hard:

During the gold rush, a man who had been mining for several months quit his job. He hadn't struck gold yet, and the work was becoming so tiring and difficult with no results. He sold his equipment to another man, who resumed mining where the first man had been left off. The new miner was advised by his engineer that there was gold worth millions only three feet away from where the first miner had stopped digging. The engineer was right, which meant the first miner was only three feet away from striking millions of dollars' worth of gold before he quit.

When things get hard, you have to work through the challenges, as nothing will come in the blink of an eye. You have to work for everything you get. The work will become difficult, hectic, and tiring, but you're closer to the finish line than you may think, and if you push just a little harder, you will succeed.

When I was young, my parents would not get me anything I wanted without me putting in work for it. I had to earn everything. So if I wanted a new phone, a bag, or a toy, I would have to do something such as receiving a better mark than I had before or finishing five books in a couple months. This built my mindset of not expecting to get what I want without earning it. I don't get anything in life without working hard for it, and to get what I want, I can't give up. I must keep going because I'm closer to the finish line than I think.

Being Blinded

I read this story online. It goes:

Once upon a time, there lived a wise man. He was the head of the local administration of a small village. Everyone respected him, and his opinions were highly regarded. His son, however, was very lazy and wasted his time sleeping and spending time with his friends. No amount of advice or threats made a difference to him. He wouldn't change at all.

As the wise man grew older, he began to worry about his son's future. He recognized the need to give something to his son so that he could take care of himself and his family in the future. One day, he called his son to his room and said, "My son, you are no longer a child. You must learn to take responsibility and understand life. I want you to find the real purpose of your life. You will lead a life full of happiness and joy." Then he handed his son a bag. When the son opened the bag, he was surprised to see four outfits, one for each season. There was also some raw food, grains, a little money, and a map.

His father continued, "I want you to go find a treasure. I have drawn a map of the place where the treasure is hidden—you need to go and find it."

The son loved this idea. The next day, he eagerly set out on a journey to find the treasure. He had to travel really far, across borders, forests, plateaus, and mountains. Days turned into weeks, and weeks turned into months. Along the way, he met a lot of people. He was helped by some with food and by some with shelter. He also came across robbers, who tried to steal from him. Slowly the season changed, and so did the landscape. When the weather was unpleasant, he halted for the day and continued his journey when the weather cleared.

Finally, after a long year, he reached his destination. It was a cliff. The map showed that the treasure was placed below the cliff under a tree. Upon spotting the tree, he began to dig into the ground. He searched and searched—around it, under it, on it—but found nothing.

He spent two days looking and digging for the treasure. By the third day, he was so exhausted that he decided to leave. Disappointed by his father's lie, he headed back to his home. On his way back, he experienced the same changing landscapes and seasons. This time, however, he halted to enjoy the blooming flowers in spring and the dancing birds in monsoon season. He stayed in places only to watch the sun set in paradise or to enjoy pleasant summer evenings.

Since the supplies he carried were gone, he learned to hunt and make arrangements for his meals. He also learned how to sew his clothes and shelter himself. He was now able to determine the hour of the day by the position of the sun and plan his journey accordingly. He learned how to protect himself from wild animals. He met the same people who had helped him earlier. This time he stayed a few days with them and helped them in some way or other to repay them. He noted how nice they were to an ordinary passerby who had nothing to offer them in return.

When he reached home, he realized it had been two years since he'd left the place. He walked straight into his father's room. "Father," he said.

The father immediately jumped to his feet and hugged his son. "So how was your journey, my son? Did you find the treasure?" he asked.

"The journey was fascinating, Father, but forgive me, for I wasn't able to find the treasure. Maybe somebody took it before I reached it." He surprised himself by what he had just said. He wasn't angry at his father. Instead, he was asking for forgiveness.

"There wasn't any treasure in the first place, my son," the father answered, smiling.

"But why did you send me to find it, then?" the son asked.

"I will surely tell you why, but first you tell me—how was your journey to the place? Did you enjoy it?"

"Of course not, Father! I had no time. I was worried someone else would find the treasure before I did. I was in a hurry to reach the cliff." He continued, "But I did enjoy the journey on my way back home. I made many friends and witnessed miracles every day. I learned so many different skills and the art of survival. There was so much I learned that it made me forget the pain of not finding the treasure."

The father said to him, "Exactly, my son. I want you to lead your life with a goal. But if you remain too focused on the goal, then you will miss out on the real treasures of life. The truth is life has no goal at all other than to just experience it to the fullest and grow every single day."

You see, life with a goal is fun, but being blinded by the goal is dangerous. The journey is important, and you will learn the most from the journey, as "it is the journey, not the destination" that holds the real prize. You have to set goals and have a purpose, but be careful, and don't get blinded by it.

Want It as Much as You Want to Breathe

You have to want it as bad as you want to breathe. *Want what?* you may ask. Your goal in life or your purpose. You have to want it to the point where you are working for it as much as you want to breathe. You have to be willing to lose sleep over it. You have to be willing to lose negative people for it. You have to be willing to lose everything for it, never stopping until you get it. Be careful: don't get blinded by it. You will lose things for it, but take the most out of the journey; it's not about the destination. When your plan doesn't work, change your plan—never change your goal.

Small Steps to Development

1. Enter a course in something you are interested in (e.g., art, coding, chess, sports).

2. Write down all your interests, and work on them one by one.

3. Work toward finding your passion.

4. Search and read about your interests.

5. Set yearly goals, and work toward them.

Change Your Mindset

The main reason so many people do not become who they want to be is because they are too attached to their old self. You hear all the time: "I've always been like this. I've always done it this way." If it works for you, keep doing it. Changing your mindset does not mean changing your personality. You have to change your view of life.

How do we change our mindset? Let's go through the steps that have helped me develop a winning mindset. Learning about different mindsets can show us how we want ours to be. Here are some things that you need to know to change your mindset:

Win-Win Attitude

Many people think that they always have to be right, and this is not true. No one is always right, and no one is perfect, we must accept that. Others believe that they're always wrong. This isn't true either. You have to have a win-win attitude.

In any disagreement, try to keep an open

mind and listen to other points of view. Find a solution that everyone can agree on—that is a win-win attitude. Having an open mind is extremely important. This means accepting other opinions and points of view and not necessarily agreeing with them. It's about listening and respecting others' opinions. This will help you understand and learn different mindsets.

Why do I need to learn other mindsets when I have my own mindset? Shouldn't I worry only about my own?

Knowing other mindsets will help you in so many ways. For one, it builds our socialization skills. We are able to expand the groups of people we interact with. Different people have different ways of socializing. Some are serious and strict; they do not like joking. Others are shy or antisocial, so you have to make the first move. Then there are those who like joking and unprofessional conversation. It's important you know how to socialize with each person. Keep in mind that no matter who you talk to, always be respectful.

I know a girl called Ghaya. Ghaya is really social and loves interacting with people. She has an amazing personality, and most people enjoy talking to her. She has a great sense of humor, but her humor is considered disrespectful by some.

One day, she met an older lady. The old lady did

not like jokes; she was straightforward and liked to be treated with respect. When the older lady and Ghaya met, Ghaya began joking around with the older lady in a disrespectful way, and the lady did not enjoy it. They left on bad terms, as the old lady addressed the unpleasant joking, and the conversation ended with the two women in a disagreement.

Do you see the importance of knowing different mindsets?

People Will Judge You No Matter What

You have to accept the fact that others won't agree with everything you do. Some people will support you no matter what. Others will always stand against you. Allow me to share a short story of my experience.

I used to put a photo of myself as the wallpaper on my phone until one of my friends said, "Mahra, no one puts their photo as a wallpaper—it's weird." At that moment, I changed my wallpaper to a celebrity's photo.

The next day, my cousins chided me with: "Who is she? No one puts a photo of other people as their wallpaper."

I changed my wallpaper once more and put a photo of New York City, and this time my brother saw it and said, "Eww! No one puts a photo of a building as their wallpaper." I was fed up and changed it to my dream car.

My friend said, "You're not a boy! Why do you have a car as your wallpaper?" By this time, I realized something. No matter what I do, some people will stand with me and others against me. I will never be able to please everyone.

What am I supposed to do, then? Please myself and ensure my own happiness. I will talk more about that in the next chapter (my favorite, by the way). Never live to please anyone but yourself, but never hurt anyone in the process.

Blame Yourself

The people who will never find success are the ones who blame others for their failures. Never blame anyone for anything in your life. It is your life, and you are the driver, so deal with your problems, and if there should be any blame to cast, blame no one but yourself. Know that it's okay to make mistakes and it is okay to fail, but it's not okay to place blame on others.

You can fix your problems and learn from them without blaming anyone. I know many people who don't accept the fact that they are wrong; they believe they are always right. (To be honest, I am sometimes like this, but I listen to what others have to say and accept that.) Apologizing is okay. There is nothing to be ashamed of when you apologize, and if you don't apologize often, get used to it. Try apologizing more. It's not a sign of weakness; it's the complete opposite. It's a sign strength.

Be Quiet

Do you want advice that will change your life? It's two simple words: *be quiet*.

Mahra, what do you mean "be quiet"? Aren't I supposed to speak out and share my thoughts? Yes, speaking in public and socializing is insanely important, but when I say "be quiet", I mean don't tell people what you are working on.

No one knows I'm writing this book except for four people: my parents, my uncle, and a trusted friend. Be careful whom you share your plans with, as not everyone has your best interests in mind. Not telling others your plan will help you; it's okay to wait until you've completed your plans.

Make it a surprise. The effect others have on you is unimaginable. I wanted to write a book years ago, but others would let me down again and again. I did not know the effect they had on me until recently. So take this advice, and whether you are working on a new business, new book, or new project, simply practice being quiet, and tell only the people who need to know. Tell them "I wrote a book" and not "I will write a book." Anyone can say "I will write a book," but not everyone can say "I wrote a book." That is the difference. People will let you down. I'll say it again: not everyone wants what's best for you, so be careful.

Don't Compare—Be You

Do not compare yourself to others, as you don't know what they are going through. I remember once a girl named Asma told me, "Mahra, look at Hour. I wish I were her." The next day Hour came up to me and said, "Mahra, look at Asma. I wish I were her." They both wanted to switch places with each other, but they didn't truly know what the other was going through.

Be grateful for who you are and what you

have, and focus on that. Nobody is perfect. You might think they are, but no one is truly perfect; you don't know what is happening in their life. Don't compare yourself to anyone but your old self. My parents would always tell me to get a better grade than I had before to get a reward—not to get a better mark than any of my siblings—and that built up my mindset to not compare myself to anyone but myself.

Don't Judge Before You Listen

Judging something from one side of the story is one of the things I hate most. When anyone tells you their point of view, always remember that it's not your place to judge. You do not know both sides of the story.

Judging anything or anyone before you are 100 percent sure is not right, and even then, it is not your place to judge. In ninth grade I transferred to a new school, and I made new friends. They told me all about these other two girls and made them look so bad, and my first impression of those other girls was that they were awful. Eventually I met the two girls my friends did not like, and they were extremely nice and respectful with high morals. I immediately knew what was going on and figured that my friends were jealous and wanted the two girls to look bad. I am now close friends with those two girls, and I learned not to judge anyone without knowing them myself.

Another time, I got into a fight with a girl— let's call her Rachel. Rachel spread a lie that

I did something I never did, and everyone in class believed her. They were against me, and I did not have the time or energy to go to each person and tell them what had really happened. Instead, I stayed quiet and moved on with my life. I couldn't make time for small-minded people who would judge others from one side of the story.

Eventually, one of them came up to me and said, "Mahra, do you know that Rachel is spreading rumors about you?"

I responded, "Yes, I do. In fact, Rachel herself came up to me and told me she is spreading rumors about me."

Then the girl said, "Then why didn't you come up to us and tell us that it is all a rumor?"

I responded, "I do not believe that it is my job to go tell everyone my side of the story. If they were wise enough, they would never judge a situation after hearing only one side of it. Besides, I know what I did, and God knows what I did; that's all I need. I don't need anyone to be on my side."

Judging before knowing both sides or before listening is like judging a perfume before smelling it. Everyone has different tastes, so try it yourself and accept the fact that everyone has different perspectives, so it is not your place to judge.

Celebrate Differences

Being different is not something to be ashamed of. This society divides us: Muslim people with Muslim people, Christian people with Christian people, Asian people with Asian people, Black people with Black people, white people with white people. This is not right. Our differences shouldn't divide us or define us. Instead, we should embrace them and make our differences bring us together, not tear us apart.

I believe that opposites attract. We all are different for a reason. We complete each other, which is why we should all work together and not let our differences stand in our way. Be different—normal is boring—and take pride in your uniqueness.

Negative Mindset

What does it mean to have a negative mindset? It is the mindset that makes you not believe in yourself. It is the mindset that will make you feel helpless and hopeless. It makes you feel like you can't; then that mindset brainwashes you into actually believing you can't when you absolutely can.

How do I control my negative mind? Did you know that saying something out loud has ten times more chance of it happening than if you just think it? Did you know that a negative thought is four to seven times more effective to your mindset than positive thoughts? Basically, voicing a negative thought has around a 70 percent chance of it coming true than if you simply said nothing. Just don't say anything negative out loud. Be careful what you say.

Trevor Moawad once told a story about a basketball player. He was interviewed at the age of twenty, and he said, "Oh, I'll play basketball, retire, then die of a heart attack at the age of forty." He eventually became a basketball player, retired, and died at the age of forty of a heart attack. Crazy, right? Everything he spoke came true. Some thoughts should be kept in your head.

Everyone Has a Point of View

Not everyone sees what you see, every person has their own point of view. Understanding that we have different viewpoints will help you out in the long run. It will also teach you that others not like you are not wrong just because they see things a different way. Listening to different people's ideas and understanding their backgrounds will allow us to see a clearer image. Imagine a world where we are all the same. How incredibly boring that would be. Why be normal when you can be different?

Do Not Return Bad Habits with Bad Habits

I always say to my siblings "لا ترد السوء بالسوء," which directly translates to "Don't return bad with bad." I like this quote, and I had never heard it before. I live by it.

A couple of days ago, I was at the park with my siblings and cousins. There were kids at the park who were trying to steal my cousin's electrical scooter. So my siblings and my cousins went to start a fight, but I was there, and I told them not to fight. They all disagreed with me and wanted to fight anyway. I told them that they did not have to respond to bad things with bad things. Their response was, "But they started it." I talked to the boys who had tried to steal their scooter, along with my siblings and cousins, and they all stopped fighting. They asked me why I had done that, and I repeated, "Do not respond to bad habits with bad habits. Always do what's right."

Paradigm

I read about the following in the book *The 7 Habits of Highly Effective Teens*. You see, sometimes we have these paradigms of things in life. What is a paradigm? A paradigm is like a perspective; it is the way you see a certain thing, your frame, reference, or belief. Paradigms are like having glasses. When you have an incomplete paradigm about anything, it is like having glasses with lenses that don't match your eyesight; those lenses affect everything you see. This makes you think that you are helping your eyesight, but you're just making it worse. The result is that what you see is what you get. If you believe you are incapable of doing certain things, your lack of belief will ensure you won't accomplish the goal.

Small Steps to Development

1. Do not to judge anyone throughout the week.

2. Next time you look in the mirror, say something nice to yourself.

3. Treat others the way you want to be treated.

4. Try not to center anyone in your life, only yourself and your principles.

5. Next time you're in a tough situa-tion, remember your principles and morals.

6. Next time someone says a bad comment about you, smile, thank them, and move on with your life.

Be Selfish

Everything is temporary. Nothing will last for-ever; the only thing you will keep for your life here on Earth is yourself. Think about that.

Be selfish. *How will that make me a better person?* You must understand that the key to self-love is being selfish. You must focus on you before you can give attention to anyone else. Take care of yourself before anyone else. Love yourself before anyone else. Help yourself before anyone else. Care about yourself before anyone else. Please yourself before anyone else. Be you, and please yourself.

Mahra, isn't that being selfish? People don't like selfish people, but being selfish isn't a bad thing. After all, it is basically putting yourself before anyone else, and there is nothing wrong with that, but I hope that by now you know that you should not worry about what others think of you. Your happiness is what matters most. You have to understand that most people want what is best for them; therefore, you must desire what is best for you. Stop thinking about *them*, and start thinking about *me*. Do not be ashamed to care about yourself; in fact, don't ever be sorry.

Don't Care What Others Think

My uncle once told this story about a teacher. The teacher answered ten complicated statistics questions on the board, and he purposely answered one of them incorrectly. All the students laughed at the teacher because he'd answered one out of the ten questions wrong. The teacher did this to teach his students a valuable life lesson—that people will always focus on the things we do wrong.

What am I supposed to do, then—become perfect? Absolutely not; you have to be happy with what you did and not let another person affect you in any way, shape, or form. Accepting others' opinions and thoughts is important. However, when they say something negative or contrary to what you know about yourself, you kindly and respectfully dismiss their comment and keep moving forward.

Always keep your head up high, and kill them with kindness, as I have said before.

Self-Love

I'll say this again. When I say *self-love*, I don't mean buying cars or having good looks, money, or high-paying jobs. Self-love is knowing your value, believing in yourself no matter what, and caring more about yourself in spite of who may or may not love you in return.

Self-love is the cure to self-hate. Love yourself too much to let others bring you down. Love yourself too much to sit with fake and toxic people. Love yourself to the point that you do not allow anyone to get too close to you or get in the way of your success. Love yourself to the point that you do not allow yourself to give up. Be goddamn selfish.

I once watched an animation of a girl who was insecure and hated herself because of what others said to her. She would cry herself to sleep every night. One day, she dreamed of her younger self and had a conversation with her. She told her younger self what she thought about her. Imagine telling your seven-year-old self that you are unloved, unsuccessful, and have no talent. The girl then realized that her whole life, every time she had been criticized, a chain would wrap itself around a part of her body. By the age of seventeen, she had so many chains, she could barely move, and realizing this broke her heart. She realized that all that had happened to her had been chained to her. She was haunted for over a decade by the mistreatment. She recognized that she had to set herself free and that loving herself would be the only way to break those chains.

Self-Reward

Many people think that self-rewarding is comical. Yet it's something people do, and it helps a lot.

How can buying yourself a gift possibly help? Self-rewarding makes you proud of yourself; it encourages you to get better. Self-rewarding is not gifting yourself whenever you feel like it. Self-rewarding is acknowledging an accomplishment. Let's say you are having trouble waking up early in the morning, so you tell yourself that if you wake up at six o'clock for a week, you will reward yourself with a trip to the spa. That will first of all help you work toward a goal, and it will encourage you to get up early in the morning.

Self-rewarding is important and is extremely helpful, because when you treat yourself, your brain releases a chemical called dopamine. This chemical makes you feel good about yourself; you become happy about meeting your goal. You are now more motivated and driven to do what you wanted to do. You are looking forward to completing the task you set for yourself.

Self-Care

Taking care of yourself requires more than bathing, eating, and getting enough sleep. Though these things are important, taking care of your mental health is too underrated, and, sadly, many people find it silly.

Going to therapy is nothing to be ashamed of, and meditating does not make you weird. I knew a girl in the seventh grade that was ashamed of going to therapy. One day, she informed me that she went to therapy because she had obsessive-compulsive disorder. She felt ashamed and was too shy to tell anyone. I immediately told her that it was fine, that going to therapy is good, and that she should not be ashamed of it. I let her know that it's a blessing and that not everyone has that mind-set to try to fix who they are. She is one of my close friends now.

The first part of recovery is admitting the fact that there is something wrong—therapy can help in this part of the process. Meditation was my savior, and many people find it odd, as though it's for people with mental health issues, but it isn't. If you haven't tried it, don't judge it, and don't try it if you don't believe in it.

I knew someone who needed help, and I wanted to help them so bad. I asked them if they would try meditation, and they said, "I am fine. I'm not sick; I don't need that silly thing you call meditation." At that point, I understood that not everyone will receive help. As much as you try to help someone, if they don't want to get better, there is nothing you can do about it.

Meditation is unbelievably helpful and has many positive qualities. First off, it will help you build a connection with yourself so that you grow to understand more of who you are. Second, it helps reduce stress and anxiety and will keep you calm. Third, it helps with self-discipline. Fourth, it reduces pain and depression, and finally, it increases memory. I can go on for months about the benefits of meditation.

Do you still think mediation is for weirdos? Well, maybe it is for weirdos, but the word *weirdo* also means *unique*—people who understand themselves. Never judge someone else's self-care practice.

Self-Discipline

The key to being successful is having self-discipline. Disciplining yourself by not allowing yourself to go to those high school parties when you should be studying for your SATs. Disciplining yourself to not go along with the troublemaking students. Disciplining is very critical to your well-being.

Having discipline will make you the person you will be in the future. The little things matter. The parties you attended mattered, the friend you went out with mattered, the sleepless celebrations mattered; every wasteful minute matters. Discipline yourself to work more, sleep less, study more, be more productive, and not go out the night before your exam or job interview.

What is the importance of self-discipline? Here is a list of things that self-disciple does.

1. Helps you achieve more in life

2. Helps with self-confidence

3. Makes you proud of yourself

4. Makes you happier with yourself

5. Helps you accomplish more

6. Provides you a better future with more success

7. Earns you others' respect and esteem

8. Leads to positive things

Don't Be Sorry

Don't be sorry for being you. Never apologize for taking care of yourself or making you important. Don't be sorry for letting go of others who held you back. Don't be sorry for not caring about others. Don't be sorry for following your dreams. Do not be sorry for doing what you have to do to have the future you want.

Be sorry for yourself for all the years you wasted on meaningless things. Be sorry for wasting many years on people who held you back. Be sorry for not caring enough about yourself. Be sorry for not loving yourself enough. Be sorry for not being selfish.

Be sorry for these things for a moment, but don't dwell on the past. Let it go!

You have to learn not to care what others think of you. Your happiness is paramount, and as long as you are not harming anyone, be all you are called to be. Not being sorry toward others and being selfish does not mean to be disrespectful or rude. Always want what's best for others, but keep yourself first. You have to help others, teach them, and respect everyone no matter what, as long as you put yourself first.

Small Steps to Development

1. Meditate.

2. Discipline yourself not to do some-
    thing you constantly do.

3. Say no to something you do not want
    to do.

4. Give yourself a day off.

5. Watch the sunrise or sunset.

6. Do something you were always
    scared to do because of others'
    judgment.

Conclusion

People will tell you, "You did your best." You are the only person who can determine that, but I know you could have done way better than you did.

How do you become the best version of yourself? I hope you took the most out of this book and learned many new things. Reread it if you need to. I hope this book helped you develop and become a better version of yourself. Remember, it is impossible to become the absolute best version of yourself.

Never forget to share your knowledge with the world, as everyone makes a difference. I wish you all the best in the future and hope to see you reading my next book, *Inshallah*. I can't wait to see you brighten the futures of the next generation. Remember you can and you will, so keep developing yourself.

In order for stars to shine, they need darkness; in order for a glow stick to glow, you need to break it, so don't expect it to be easy work. Work through the obstacles and become a better person with higher goals. Don't listen to the haters; instead, prove them wrong. No matter who they are, friend or even family, believe in yourself as I believe in you.

Congratulations, you finished reading this book. I hope it inspired you and helped you develop and become a person you are proud of. Keep going and never stop the grind. We all have our good days and bad days, and it's okay to take a break, give yourself a chance to rest, but don't make it a habit. No matter what you're going through, make sure to be you and embrace that, do what makes you happy, and take care of yourself not only physically but mentally as well. Do not put yourself in a position to get hurt. Most importantly, don't stop here. Continue your reading journey, as this is only the beginning, and there's so much more out there. I wish you the best of luck in the future, and I am sure you will become a successful and impactful person.

Book Study Guide

Be Productive and Don't Procrastinate

1. What is procrastination?

2. How do I get over procrastination?

3. How do you procrastinate, and how can you get over it?

Make Mistakes and Take Risks

1. Why is making mistakes important?

2. Why should you take risks?

3. When did you take risks and make mistakes, and what did you learn from it?

Know Your Worth

1. What is your worth?

2. How can you know your worth?

3. What do you do when you are in a place that doesn't know your worth?

Let Go

1. What is the importance of letting go?

2. Who did you let go of?

3. How did you let go?

Live Life with Passion

1. What is your passion?

2. Why do you want to know your passion?

3. How will knowing your passion help you?

Change Your Mindset

1. Why is understanding other mind-sets a blessing?

2. Why is it important to change your mindset?

3. How did you change your mindset?

Be Selfish

1. What does it mean to be selfish?

2. How can you become selfish?

3. What will being selfish help you with?

Acknowledgments

Thanks to every person that was a part of my life, whether you had a good or bad effect on it; I want to thank every single person. A special thank-you to those who helped me through my hard times, even if it was for a short period of time. Thanks to my family, my parents, my aunt and uncles, and my friends. Thanks to myself as well, for working hard, believing in myself, working through obstacles, and never giving up despite all the hard times.

Bibliography

Way #3

https://www.jeremyanderson.org, speech by Jeremy Anderson about the dollar bill

https://youtu.be/BQcp1ZNWgTs, carpenter story

Way #4

https://youtu.be/UwHhxeaSSRM, snake and the saw

https://kottke.org/20/01/the-story-of-two-monks-and-a-woman, monks

https://madamsabi.wordpress.com/2015/06/29/the-three-analogy-of-the-three-types-of-people-in-your-life-by-tyler-perry/, types of people

https://www.inspirationalstories.eu/stories-about-letting-go-of-the-past/, bird story

Way #5

https://www.forbes.com/sites
/margiewarrell/2013/10/30
/know-your-why-4-questions-to-tap-the
-power-of-purpose/?sh=1f5452d173ad,
purpose questions

https://maglite.com/blogs
/maghistory-blog-1/the-lion-and-the-gazelle,
lion and gazelle story

https://myhappydigitallifestyle.com
/the-journey-is-the-real-treasure-not-the
-destination/, father and son story

Way #7

https://youtu.be/V6ui161NyTg, short animation about self-love

About the Author

Mahra Ali Alali

Mahra is a thirteen-year-old author. She has been an avid chess player from the age of three, and she is also a horse rider.

Mahra was born into a family of writers. The author also takes Spanish classes and is currently at the third level.

She loves helping others and has had experience with self-help. She has had to figure out how to help herself, and now she wants to help others.

Mahra is also a frequent reader and loves reading self-help books. She reads about one book every month.

She has huge ambitions, and this is just the beginning for her.

About the Publisher

The Dreamwork Collective is a print and digital publisher sharing diverse voices and powerful stories with the world. Dedicated to the advancement of humanity, we strive to create books that have a positive impact on people and on the planet. Our hope is that our books document this moment in time for future generations to enjoy and learn from, and that we play our part in ushering humanity into a new era of heightened creativity, connection, and compassion.

www.thedreamworkcollective.com

@thedreamworkcollective